JEHOVAH'S
WITNESSES

by Harold J. Berry
Professor of Bible and Greek
Grace College of the Bible
Omaha, Nebraska

BACK TO THE BIBLE
LINCOLN, NE 68501

369,000 printed to date—1995
(1155-038—14M—45)
ISBN 0-8474-0818-3

Printed in the United States of America

JEHOVAH'S WITNESSES

Few people in the United States have not been called on at least once by the Jehovah's Witnesses. These door-to-door evangelists are members of one of the most aggressive religious groups in the world. In 1975 the Jehovah's Witnesses numbered 554,257 in 6542 congregations in the United States. By 1988 their membership had increased to 752,404 in 8336 congregations.[1] While the Jehovah's Witnesses do not maintain actual membership lists, their worldwide membership is now estimated to be 2.2 million.[2]

Despite the lack of welcome they receive in many homes, the Jehovah's Witnesses determinedly march on to the next house. Those who talk with the

Jehovah's Witnesses soon realize that their beliefs differ greatly from those of historic Christianity. What causes this group to be so aggressive in its witnessing? And where did its unusual beliefs originate?

Background

The first recognized leader—and first president—of the Jehovah's Witnesses was Charles Taze Russell. Born in what is now Pittsburgh, Pennsylvania, on February 16, 1852, Russell had a Congregational and Presbyterian upbringing. However, he became opposed to organized religion and to many of the teachings of historic Christianity. "By his own admission, it was the Adventists who delivered Russell from his early skepticism," Anthony Hoekema wrote. "From the Adventists Russell obviously borrowed such doctrines as the extinction of the soul at death, the annihilation of the wicked, the denial of hell, and a modified form of the investigative judgment."[3]

Many Jehovah's Witnesses and Seventh-day Adventists have denied this association with the teachings of Adventism. However, J. K. Van Baalen wrote: "The origin of the Russell-Rutherford-Knorr theology, especially of its eschatology, lies in Seventh-day Adventism. This was asserted in *The Chaos of Cults* in 1929, hotly disclaimed by LeRoy E. Froom, and has since been reaffirmed by Lehman Strauss, F. E. Mayer, and E. C. Gruss."[4]

His "faith" renewed, Russell organized a Bible class in Pittsburgh in 1870. This group met regularly to study the Scriptures about Jehovah's Kingdom and the Second Coming of Christ. Even though Russell was still a teenager and had no formal theological training, he became the undisputed leader of the group.

In 1879 Russell began a magazine entitled *Zion's Watch Tower and Herald of Christ's Presence,* since renamed *The Watchtower Announcing Jehovah's Kingdom.* It is commonly known as *The Watchtower.* This magazine is the group's main source of teaching and is considered to be authoritative by its members. Since its inception, the publication has grown tremendously. According to the February 1, 1984, issue of *The Watchtower,* the average number printed each issue is 10,200,000 and it is now published in 102 languages.[5] *Awake!* another popular magazine published by the Jehovah's Witnesses, is printed in many languages each month with circulation in the millions.

The Jehovah's Witnesses was incorporated in Pennsylvania in 1884 under the name Zion's Watch Tower Tract Society. The group officially adopted the name Jehovah's Witnesses in 1931. This name is derived from the American Standard Version translation of Isaiah 43:12: "Ye are my witnesses, saith Jehovah, and I am God." In addition, the group has also been commonly known as the Russellites.

Russell was involved in many conflicts during his life. The integrity and stability of his life were less than admirable. In 1913 the courts granted his wife a divorce, and he was charged with fraud and perjury. Walter Martin has reproduced many of these records in his outstanding work, *The Kingdom of the Cults.*[6] Concerning this first leader of the Jehovah's Witnesses, Martin stated, "As a speaker, Russell swayed many, as a theologian, he impressed no one competent; as a man, he failed before the true God."[7]

After the death of Russell in 1916, the group was led by "Judge" Joseph F. Rutherford, who had been the society's legal counselor since 1907. Rutherford was even more strongly opposed to organized religion than Russell had been. He was a prolific writer and ruled the group with an iron hand. Under his leadership, the Jehovah's Witnesses began their strong emphasis on door-to-door visitation and literature distribution.

Following Rutherford's death in 1942, he was succeeded by Nathan H. Knorr. Since 1942, the organization has grown at a phenomenal rate. Knorr was responsible for improving the group's training program and for producing a vast amount of literature, including the translation and publication of their "official" version of the Bible, the *New World Translation of the Holy Scriptures*. The current president is Frederick W. Franz, who succeeded Knorr in 1977.

Beliefs

The Jehovah's Witnesses are probably best known for some of their practices. They are pacifists and refuse to serve in their country's military. They also do not salute their country's flag or celebrate Christmas, birthdays and other holidays because they believe these are forms of idolatry. In addition, they will not accept blood transfusions for themselves or members of their family because they think this violates the Old Testament prohibition against eating blood.

But even more important than their practices are the doctrines they teach and believe. What is the source of authority for the Jehovah's Witnesses and what are their beliefs?

Source of Authority

The Jehovah's Witnesses claim the Bible is their final authority. In their book *Let God Be True* the writer stated, "To let God be found true means to let God have the say as to what is the truth that sets men free. It means to accept his

Word, the Bible, as the truth. . . . Our obligation is to back up what is said herein by quotations from the Bible for proof of truthfulness and reliability."[8] But is this claim followed?

When talking with the Jehovah's Witnesses, one soon learns that the interpretations of their leaders are considered to be the final authority, not the Bible itself. In *The Watchtower,* September 15, 1910, page 298, Russell stated, "If the six volumes of 'Scripture Studies' are practically the Bible, topically arranged with Bible proof texts given, we might not improperly name the volumes 'The Bible in an Arranged Form.' That is to say, they are not mere comments on the Bible, but they are practically the Bible itself. Furthermore, not only do we find that people cannot see the divine plan in studying the Bible by itself, but we see, also, that if anyone lays the 'Scripture Studies' aside, even after he has used them, . . . and goes to the Bible alone, though he has understood his Bible for ten years, our experience shows that within two years, he goes into darkness. On the other hand, if he had merely read the 'Scripture Studies' with their references and had not read a page of the Bible as such, he would be in the light at the end of two years, because he would have the light of the Scriptures."[9]

Thus, the Jehovah's Witnesses believe that the writings of Russell and Rutherford take precedence over the Bible. *Studies in the Scriptures* and Russell's other books still remain the primary source of authority. When the Jehovah's Witnesses use the Bible, they refer to their own version—the *New World Translation* (NWT). First published in 1950, this translation contains many changes in the wording of key passages that reflect the binding interpretations of the group's leaders. So the leader's interpretation of the Bible, not the Bible itself, is the final authority for the Jehovah's Witnesses.

Trinity

The biblical teachings concerning the Trinity are vital in understanding the doctrinal errors of the Jehovah's Witnesses. The Witnesses emphatically deny the trinitarian view of God. They believe that God is only the "Jehovah God" referred to in the Old Testament; they deny the concept of one God who exists in three distinct persons—Father, Son and Spirit—that the Bible teaches. The Jehovah's Witnesses claim that trinitarianism is a belief in three gods, which is polytheism.

The Jehovah's Witnesses and others who deny that God is a trinity frequently cite Deuteronomy 6:4 as proof of their views. This verse says, "Hear, O Israel: The Lord our God is one Lord." However, the Hebrew word translated "one" in this passage does not refer to an absolute unity but to a composite unity. This is the same word used in Genesis 2:24 to describe the marriage relationship. Here the husband and wife are said to be "one flesh." Therefore, Deuteronomy 6:4 in no way excludes the Trinity; rather, the Hebrew word used for "one" indicates that more than one person is being referred to. The plural pronouns used for God also give evidence of the Trinity (see Gen. 1:26; 11:7).

The existence of the Trinity is revealed

to us in the Bible; however, our limited minds often find this doctrine difficult to comprehend. It has been stated in this way: "While God is one, He exists as three persons. These persons are equal, have the same attributes, and are equally worthy of adoration, worship and faith."[10]

The Jehovah's Witnesses denial of the Trinity is essentially Arianism, a heresy that was condemned in the fourth century by the Council of Nicea. In rejecting the Trinity, the Jehovah's Witnesses de-emphasize the Person of Christ by denying His deity.

Jesus Christ

Because they deny the doctrine of the Trinity, the Jehovah's Witnesses do not believe that Jesus Christ is God. As a result, they add this view to their translation of the Bible wherever they are able to fit it in. Commenting on Colossians 1:15, they say of Christ, "Thus he is ranked with God's creation, being first among them and also most beloved and most favored among them. He is not the author of the creation of God; but, after God had created him as his firstborn

Son, then God used him as his working Partner in the creating of all the rest of creation. It is so stated at Colossians 1:16-18 and at John 1:1-3, *NW*."[11]

The Jehovah's Witnesses frequently cite passages from Colossians and the Gospel of John to prove that Jesus Christ is not God. In examining their teachings, it is important to note how the *New World Translation* renders these vital passages.

Colossians 1:16,17 states, "Because by means of him all [other] things were created in the heavens and upon the earth, the things visible and the things invisible, no matter whether they are thrones or lordships or governments or authorities. All [other] things have been created through him and for him. Also he is before all [other] things and by means of him all [other] things were made to exist" (NWT).[12]

These verses serve as a key example of the extent to which the Jehovah's Witnesses will go to support their belief that Jesus Christ is not God. They have even changed the translation of the Bible. The original Greek text contains

13

no word that could be translated "other" in this passage, yet they have added the word four times in these two verses. The original version of the *New World Translation* did not contain the brackets around the word "other" to show that it was not part of the original Greek. The Jehovah's Witnesses have since added the brackets with this explanation: "Brackets enclose words inserted to complete the sense in the English text."[13]

However, as any Greek student knows, there is no basis for the assumption that the word "other" is needed to complete the sense in this passage. They have inserted this word to prevent the text from saying that Jesus Christ created all things. To allow the Bible to say that Jesus created *all* things would destroy their teaching that Christ was created by Jehovah. Thus, He could create only "other" things.

Although the Jehovah's Witnesses insert the word "other" into the *New World Translation,* the *Emphatic Diaglott*—a Greek-English interlinear version to which they like to refer—does not include the word "other" in the

Greek text or in the English translation of this passage.[14] Clearly, the *New World Translation* passes on an interpretation that is not based on the original language of the New Testament. The Greek text of Colossians 1:16,17—including the *Emphatic Diaglott* of the Jehovah's Witnesses—clearly states that Jesus Christ created all things, serving as indisputable proof that He is God.

Jehovah's Witnesses are also fond of taking advantage of people's ignorance of the original language in their reference to John 1:1. The *New World Translation* renders this verse: "In [the] beginning the Word was, and the Word was with God, and the Word was a god." The Witnesses have added the word "a" in front of "god" in order to support their belief that Jesus Christ is not Jehovah God.

The Greek language uses only the definite article (the). When no article appears, one must decide whether or not to supply the indefinite article (a). The Jehovah's Witnesses, however, have gone beyond the rules of Greek grammar to support their theology. The elementary Greek grammar book, *Essentials of New Testament Greek*, states that when the definite article appears with a word, it emphasizes identity. When the article does not appear, it indicates "quality or characteristics."[15] Therefore, in terms of quality, the Word was God; that is, Jesus Christ is deity.

The debated phrase in John 1:1 has two nouns—"God" and "Word." According to the rules of Greek grammar, when only one noun has the definite article in this kind of construction, it is the subject of the sentence. The noun without the article is the predicate (it makes a statement about the subject). Thus, the proper translation of this verse is "The Word was God."

The Jehovah's Witnesses are inconsistent in their handling of the Greek New Testament. They are quick to supply the indefinite article (a) in John 1:1 to back up their teaching that Jesus is not God. But in verses 6, 12, 13 and 18 of the same chapter, the word "God" does not contain an article, yet they do not supply the indefinite article in these passages.

The Jehovah's Witnesses are also inconsistent regarding their own teachings. They claim to worship only one God, while accusing trinitarians of being polytheistic. Yet, by insisting that John 1:1 should be translated, "The Word was a god," they are in fact guilty of polytheism—they consider Jesus Christ to be *one* of the gods.

Any Greek student could give example after example of how the Jehovah's Witnesses have misused the Greek language. The heart of the issue, however, is not their misuse of Greek but the fact that they are adding their own interpretations to the Bible in order to support their faulty theology. But the Christian can be assured that every argument of the Jehovah's Witnesses from the Greek text can be answered by those believers who know Greek well. The false doctrines of this cult cannot stand in the light of the Scriptures.

Use of the Name Jehovah

The Jehovah's Witnesses try so hard to distinguish between Jesus and Jehovah God that they do not notice how their own translation reveals that Jesus is Jehovah. Isaiah 40:3 says, "The voice of him that crieth in the wilderness, Prepare ye the way of the Lord, make straight in the desert a highway for our God." The Hebrew word translated "Lord" in this verse is the one from which "Jehovah" is derived. This verse is a commonly accepted prophecy about the first coming of the Lord Jesus Christ, as announced by John the Baptist.

All four Gospel accounts allude to the fact that Jesus is the fulfillment of Isaiah 40:3. Notice how the *New World Translation* renders the various verses: "This, in fact, is the one spoken of through Isaiah the prophet in these words: 'Listen! Someone is crying out in the wilderness, "Prepare the way of Jehovah, YOU people! Make his roads straight"'" (Matt. 3:3).

Mark 1:1-3 especially pinpoints Jesus Christ as the fulfillment of Isaiah's prophecy. The *New World Translation* says, "[The] beginning of the good news about Jesus Christ: Just as it is written in Isaiah the prophet: '(Look! I am sending

18

forth my messenger before your face, who will prepare your way;) listen! someone is crying out in the wilderness, "Prepare the way of Jehovah, YOU people, make his roads straight." ' "

Luke 3:4 and John 1:23 contain similar statements, showing that Jesus indeed is the fulfillment of Isaiah's prophecy. Thus, when John the Baptist was preparing the way for Jesus Christ, he was in reality preparing for the arrival of Jehovah on earth. Once again the Witnesses' own translation contradicts their teaching that Jesus Christ is not God.

Resurrection of Christ

In addition to holding erroneous views about the Person of Christ, the Jehovah's Witnesses also teach false doctrine concerning His resurrection. In *Let God Be True*, they stated, "God did not purpose for Jesus to be humiliated thus forever by being a fleshly man forever. No, but after he had sacrificed his perfect manhood, God raised him to deathless life as a glorious spirit creature. He exalted him above all angels and other

19

parts of God's universal organization, to be next-highest to himself, the Most High God."[16] Notice their claim that Jesus was raised from the dead as a "glorious spirit creature."

This is not what the Bible teaches. After the resurrection of Christ, the Scriptures record that Mary Magdalene mistakenly thought He was the gardener (see John 20:15). The Lord Jesus Christ also invited Thomas to feel the wounds in His side and hands (see v. 27). These and other passages show that the resurrected Christ had a physical body.

The Jehovah's Witnesses explain all of this away by saying that Jesus "materialized" at various times so He could be seen alive, even though He did not have a physical body. Such a view distorts the normal sense of the Scriptures. It is another evidence that the Jehovah's Witnesses follow their leaders' interpretations more than they do the teachings of the Bible. The main point of I Corinthians 15—a central passage on the resurrection—is that the physical resurrection of Christ assures believers of a physical resurrection.

The Holy Spirit

Since the Jehovah's Witnesses deny the Trinity and the deity of Christ, it is no surprise that they reject the deity of the Holy Spirit as well. Concerning the Holy Spirit, they wrote: "So the holy spirit is the invisible active force of Almighty God which moves his servants to do his will."[17] Not only do the Jehovah's Witnesses deny that the Holy Spirit is God, but they do not even believe He is a person.

However, the Scriptures teach us that the Holy Spirit is not a "force"; He is a person who possesses intellect, emotions and will. He does things only a person can do. He reproves the world of sin, of righteousness and of judgment (John 16:8), He teaches (14:26), He regenerates (3:6), He baptizes (I Cor. 12:13), and He can be grieved (Eph. 4:30).

Salvation

According to the Jehovah's Witnesses, salvation is a reward for good works. In *Let God Be True* they expressed this belief: "All who by reason of faith in

21

Jehovah God and in Christ Jesus dedicate themselves to do God's will and then faithfully carry out their dedication will be rewarded with everlasting life (Romans 6:23). However, that life will not be the same for all. The Bible plainly shows that some of these, that is, 144,000, will share in heavenly glory with Christ Jesus, while the others will enjoy the blessings of life down here on earth (Revelation 14:1,3; Micah 4:1-5)."[18]

From this statement we see why the Jehovah's Witnesses evidence such great zeal in spreading their teaching from house to house—they are doing it to earn salvation. They teach a salvation by works, not by faith.

Once again the Jehovah's Witnesses have departed from historic Christianity in their doctrines regarding the means of salvation. They see works as being part of the requirements for obtaining salvation rather than being a result of salvation. The Bible clearly states the means of salvation in Ephesians 2:8,9. Even the *New World Translation* renders these two verses so clearly that Witnesses would change their theology if they took them seriously: "By this undeserved kindness, indeed, YOU have been saved through faith; and this not owing to YOU, it is God's gift. No, it is not owing to works, in order that no man should have ground for boasting."

When Jesus Christ shed His blood on the cross, He propitiated (satisfied) God's demand for righteousness. As a result, all who place their faith in Jesus Christ have the benefits of His death applied to them. They are justified, or declared righteous, before God.

Because the Jehovah's Witnesses believe that a person is "rewarded with everlasting life," they teach that a person does not know until death whether or not he has done enough to be rewarded with everlasting life. How many good works and door-to-door contacts does it take for a person to merit God's favor? According to the Bible, a believer can know for sure he has everlasting life from the moment of his salvation. This is made clear even in the Jehovah's Witnesses' own translation: "And this is the witness given, that God gave us everlasting life, and this life is in his Son. He that

23

has the Son has this life; he that does not have the Son of God does not have this life. I write YOU these things that YOU may know that YOU have life everlasting, YOU who put YOUR faith in the name of the Son of God" (I John 5:11-13, NWT).

So once again we see that the doctrine of salvation taught by the Jehovah's Witnesses not only contradicts the Bible's teachings but is not even in agreement with key passages in their own translation.

Soul Sleep

The Jehovah's Witnesses—along with the Seventh-day Adventists and the Worldwide Church of God—teach that when a believer dies, he remains in an unconscious state of existence in the grave until he is resurrected by God. The Jehovah's Witnesses do not believe the soul of a person is a separate entity that has consciousness.

The Bible teaches, however, that man is a triune being. He possesses a body, a soul and a spirit—each separate from the others. When the body dies, the soul and spirit do not cease to exist but are merely separated from the body. Matthew 10:28 says, "And fear not them which kill the body, but are not able to kill the soul: but rather fear him which is able to destroy both soul and body in hell."

Luke 16:19-31 offers proof of a conscious existence after death. This account tells of a rich man and a beggar by the name of Lazarus. Because Lazarus had believed in God during his lifetime, he was in a conscious state of bliss after physical death. The rich man, on the other hand, had rejected God and thus was in a conscious state of torment. The rich man not only was conscious, but he also retained his memory of his life on earth. He remembered his five brothers and wanted Abraham to send Lazarus to warn them about the place of torment. Thus, we see from this passage that both the saved and unsaved are in a conscious state after physical death.

While the Jehovah's Witnesses often point to a number of Old Testament passages to substantiate their teachings regarding soul sleep, nowhere in the Bible do we find this idea expressed. The Apostle Paul recognized no middle ground between this life and the next. He knew that at the moment of death, he would immediately be with the Lord Jesus: "I say, [I am] willing rather to be absent from the body, and to be present with the Lord" (II Cor. 5:8).

First Thessalonians 4:14 states conclusively that believers are not in an unconscious state in the grave while they are waiting for the resurrection. This is seen even in the *New World Translation*: "For if our faith is that Jesus died and rose again, so, too, those who have fallen asleep [in death] through Jesus God will bring with him." Notice where the believers are. Even though their bodies are in the grave, the real persons—the souls and spirits of departed believers—are with Christ and come back with Him at His appearance. When Christ returns, the bodies of believers will be resurrected from the grave and united with their souls and spirits. If believers were in an unconscious state in the grave, it would be impossible for God to bring them back with Him.

The Scriptures teach that even though the believer's body remains in the grave at death, his soul and spirit go directly to be with Christ. On the other hand, the soul and spirit of the unbeliever experiences torment after death.

Annihilation of the Wicked

Like many cults, the Jehovah's Witnesses also teach that the wicked will not be punished forever but will be annihilated.

According to the Jehovah's Witnesses, "the doctrine of a burning hell where the wicked are tortured eternally after death cannot be true, mainly for four reasons: (1) It is wholly unscriptural; (2) it is unreasonable; (3) it is contrary to God's love; and (4) it is repugnant to justice."[19]

The doctrine of a burning hell is not unscriptural or unreasonable unless a person reads the Bible with his conclusions already drawn regarding what is reasonable. Actually, it is unreasonable to think that God would extend His grace and forgiveness to everyone who

27

trusts in Jesus Christ for salvation, but the Bible reveals that He does.

An eternal hell is not contrary to God's love. Instead, its existence helps explain why God exercised His love by sending His Son to die on the cross so people might receive Him as Saviour and escape the burning hell. If the doctrine of hell is unreasonable, why then don't the Jehovah's Witnesses say it is contrary to God's love to require His Son to suffer agony and death on the cross for sin?

Likewise, the doctrine of a burning hell is not repugnant to justice. God has given man his choice either to believe in Christ by faith for the forgiveness of sin or to refuse to trust in Christ and spend eternity in hell. We choose the judgment we will receive. What could be more just?

According to the Bible, a person cannot claim everlasting life for the believer unless he claims everlasting punishment for the unbeliever. In referring to those whom the Lord will judge when He returns to earth, Matthew 25:46 concludes: "And these shall go away into everlasting punishment: but the righteous into life eternal."

The Jehovah's Witnesses and others who believe in the annihilation of the wicked have tried to make a distinction between the words "everlasting" and "eternal" in this passage. They teach that the "everlasting punishment" refers to the fact that the wicked will be cut off from God forever; however, they will not endure eternal torment but will instead be immediately annihilated. But this supposition is not supported in the original language. These words are merely two translations of the same Greek word—their meaning is the same. Once again, the Jehovah's Witnesses have attempted to distort the normal sense of the Scriptures in order to support their faulty theology.

A comparison of two verses in the Book of the Revelation sheds additional light on the eternal state of unbelievers. At the end of the Tribulation, two individuals known as "the beast" and "the false prophet" will be "cast alive into a lake of fire burning with brimstone" (19:20). Following this event, Christ will reign on earth for 1000 years (see 20:1-6). During a "little season" at the end of this 1000-year period, Satan will be loosed from the bondage he was in during the Millennium and will gather a group to fight against God and His armies (see vv. 7-9). Satan and his forces will be defeated at that time. Then, according to Revelation 20:10, "the devil that deceived them was cast into the lake of fire and brimstone, where the beast and the false prophet are, and shall be tormented day and night for ever and ever." Although 1000 years will have passed, the beast and the false prophet will still be in the lake of fire. They have not been annihilated.

Prophecy

The Watchtower Society is a date-setting organization. They believe that God still makes new revelations through "prophets" today. In the eyes of the Jehovah's Witnesses, a false prophet is a person who prophesies something that does not occur. By this definition, they are guilty of being false prophets many times over.

However, while they have frequently given false predictions of events, they have later managed to explain away the false prophecies by fanciful spiritualizing. Some of these attempts to set dates (and later to reinterpret them when they didn't occur) include: The invisible Second Coming of Jesus in 1874; the end of the world in 1914 and again in 1975; the prediction that all members of the Body of Christ would be changed to heavenly glory in 1925; and that World War II was Armageddon.[20]

After examining the above predictions from the Watchtower Society, Duane Magnani—himself a former Jehovah's Witness for 18 years—said, "The record clearly destroys any claims to the prophetic authority of the Watchtower Bible and Tract Society."[21]

Ed Gruss, also a former Jehovah's Witness, examined predictions of the Watchtower Society back to 1877. He concluded, "When I looked at the many events the Jehovah's Witnesses had predicted and the specific dates they had set, I found that in *every case* the prediction had proved to be false" [italics his].[22]

Even though their predictions that the world would end in 1914 and again in 1975 were erroneous, the Jehovah's Witnesses still have not given up their date-setting practices. They again predicted that the world would end in 1984. Gary and Heather Botting have exposed the group's false prophecies in their book, *The Orwellian World of Jehovah's Witnesses* (University of Toronto Press).[23]

Conclusion

As we have seen from this brief study, the Jehovah's Witnesses deny many fundamentals of the Christian faith, including the deity of the Lord Jesus Christ. A closer look at their doctrines reveals many other areas in which they have departed from the Bible's teachings. For this reason, they cannot be considered "Christians" in the scriptural sense of the word. While we may admire their dedication and enthusiasm toward their beliefs, their zeal and sincerity are not acceptable before God as substitutes for doing His will and teaching His truth. Like the Jews of Paul's day, the Jehovah's Witnesses "have a zeal of God, but not according to knowledge" (Rom. 10:2).

Notes

[1] *The World Almanac and Book of Facts, 1976* and *1989* (New York: Newspaper Enterprise Association, Inc.), p. 488 and p. 590.

[2] *The World Book Encyclopedia*, 1986, Vol. 11, p. 70.

[3] Anthony A. Hoekema, *Four Major Cults* (Grand Rapids: Wm. B. Eerdmans Publishing Company, 1963), p. 224.

[4] J. K. Van Baalen, *The Chaos of Cults*, 4th rev. ed.; (Grand Rapids: Wm. B. Eerdmans Publishing Company, 1962), p. 257.

[5] *The Watchtower Announcing Jehovah's Kingdom*, Feb. 1, 1984, p. 2.

[6] Walter Martin, *The Kingdom of the Cults*, 3rd rev. ed.; (Minneapolis: Bethany House Publishers, 1985), pp. 39-45.

[7] *Ibid.*, p. 45.

[8]*Let God Be True,* 2nd ed.; (Brooklyn: Watch Tower Bible and Tract Society, 1952), p. 9.

[9]*The Watchtower,* Sept. 15, 1910, p. 298, cited by Walter Martin, *The Kingdom of the Cults,* p. 46, and by Anthony Hoekema, *Four Major Cults,* p. 227.

[10]Lewis Sperry Chafer, *Major Bible Themes,* rev. by John F. Walvoord (Grand Rapids: Zondervan Publishing House, 1974), p. 40.

[11]*Let God Be True,* p. 33.

[12]*New World Translation of the Holy Scriptures* (Brooklyn: Watchtower Bible and Tract Society of New York, Inc., 1961).

[13]*Ibid.,* p. 6.

[14]*The Emphatic Diaglott,* rev. ed.; (Brooklyn: International Bible Students Association Watch Tower Bible and Tract Society, 1942).

[15]Ray Summers, *Essentials of New Testament Greek* (Nashville: Broadman Press, 1950), p. 16.

[16]*Let God Be True,* p. 41.

[17]*Ibid.,* p. 108.

[18]*Ibid.,* p. 298.

[19]*Ibid.,* p. 99.

[20]For documentation of the Jehovah's Witnesses' claims see Duane Magnani, *The Watchtower Files,* rev. ed.; (Minneapolis: Bethany House Publishers, 1985), pp. 63-99.

[21]*Ibid.,* p. 67.

[22]Dave Hunt, *The Cult Explosion* (Eugene, OR: Harvest House Publishers, 1980), p. 208.

[23]Religious News Service, "Do Jehovah's Witnesses Still Hold to Their 1984 Doomsday Deadline?" *Christianity Today,* Sept. 21, 1984, pp. 66,67.

Summary

Name of Organization: Watch Tower Bible and Tract Society
Also known as: Jehovah's Witnesses

Founder: Charles Taze Russell (1852-1916)

Current President: Frederick W. Franz

Headquarters: Brooklyn, New York

Membership (1988): U.S.: 752,404   Worldwide: 2.2 million

Beliefs

	Page(s)
Source of Authority	
Claim the Bible is their final authority.	8,9
Russell's writings, especially *Studies in the Scriptures*, are considered "the light of the Scriptures"	9,10
Have their own translation (*New World Translation*), which reflects leaders' views	10
The Watchtower magazine is one of their main sources of doctrine.	5,6
Trinity	
Believe that God is not a trinity but only "Jehovah God" . . .	10-12

Jesus Christ

Use of Name Jehovah

Resurrection of Christ

Say Christ was resurrected as a "glorious spirit creature" and did not have a physical body 19,20

Claim Jesus "materialized" so He could be seen alive 20

The Holy Spirit

Deny He is third person of the Trinity 21

Claim He is only an "active force" 21

Salvation

Claim everlasting life is a reward for doing the will of God and carrying out one's dedication 21,22

Recommended Reading

Enroth, Ronald, and others. *A Guide to Cults and New Religions.* Downers Grove, IL: InterVarsity Press, 1983.

Hoekema, Anthony A. *Four Major Cults.* Grand Rapids: Wm. B. Eerdmans Publishing Company, 1963.

Magnani, Duane, and Barrett, Arthur. *The Watchtower Files: Dialogue With a J.W.* Minneapolis: Bethany House Publishers, 1985.

Martin, Walter R. *The Kingdom of the Cults.* Minneapolis: Bethany House Publishers, 1965, 1977, 1985.

McDowell, Josh, and Stewart, Don. *Handbook of Today's Religions.* San Bernardino, CA: Here's Life Publishers, Inc., 1983.

Passantino, Robert; Passantino, Gretchen; and Oehm, Ray. *Answers to the Cultist at Your Door.* Eugene, OR: Harvest House Publishers, 1981.

Van Baalen, J. K. *The Chaos of Cults.* Grand Rapids: Wm. B. Eerdmans Publishing Company, 1962.

Back to the Bible is a nonprofit ministry dedicated to Bible teaching, evangelism and edification of Christians worldwide.

If we may assist you in knowing more about Christ and the Christian life, please write to us without obligation:

Back to the Bible
P.O. Box 82808
Lincoln, NE 68501